English 3

C000229047

Practice in the Basic Skills

Contents

Verbs (1)

A Write down a word which shows how each of the following moves.

1   yourself   _walk_   6   a horse   _gallop_

2   a dog   _runs_   7   a rabbit   _hops_

3   a snake   _slithers_   8   a swallow   _swoops_

4   a cat   ~~jumps~~ _skips_   9   a salmon   _swims_

5   a frog   _jumps_   10   a monkey   _climbs_

B Write down a word which shows how each of the following moves.

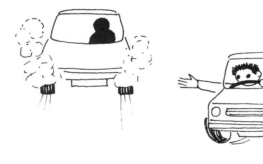 

1   a car   _drives_   6   water   _runs_

2   leaves   _fall_   7   an elephant   _stamps_

3   a ball   _bounces_   8   a kite   _swoops_

4   grass   _blowing_   9   snow   _falling_

5   an aeroplane   _fly_   10   a clown   _sillily_

Nouns

A   Write out the **nouns** in each of these sentences.

  1   The horse was old.

  2   I like chocolate.

  3   The water is cold.

  4   This apple is sour.

  5   We ate our dinner.

  6   The police officer caught the thief.

  7   The cat climbed on the roof.

  8   The boys and girls went to the cinema.

  9   Leaves fell from the tree.

  10 There are many books in the library.

B   Write down three things you might see:

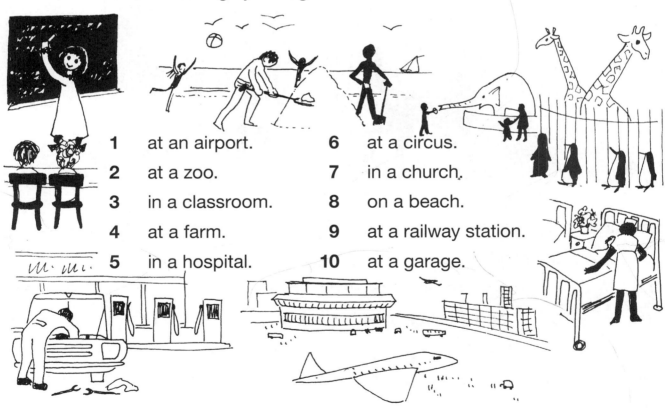

  1   at an airport.   **6**   at a circus.

  2   at a zoo.   **7**   in a church.

  3   in a classroom.   **8**   on a beach.

  4   at a farm.   **9**   at a railway station.

  5   in a hospital.   **10** at a garage.

C   Write the names of:

  1   five flowers.   **2**   five birds.   **3**   five trees.

Picture comprehension (1)

Write out the story filling in the twelve spaces by choosing your own words.

Sam and Paul _____ the fence. They couldn't wait to get into the

_____ to enjoy the _____ . They climbed up to a thick _____

and _____ many apples. They also enjoyed _____ them! Soon they

saw a _____ dog looking up at them and _____ . The boys were

very _____ and daren't _____ . Things became worse, for it was

now _____ and the dog was still there. Also, walking towards the tree was

the _____ .

Now write what you think happened next.

Punctuation

A   Write a sentence about each picture.

Remember **capital letters** and **full stops**.

B   Write out these sentences putting in a **full stop** or a **question mark** at the end of each.

1   The Jumbo jet landed safely

2   Have you seen our new caretaker

3   A tortoise has a hard shell

4   We enjoyed Tim's party

5   Will you play football with me

6   Did you see that unusual bird

7   Our lawn needs cutting

8   Why don't you eat your dinner

C   Write out these sentences, putting in the missing **commas**.

1   The butcher sells lamb, beef, chicken, and sausages.

2   The cricket season is May, June, July, August, and September.

3   The sailor had been to China Japan India and Australia.

4   I saw snowdrops crocuses daffodils and tulips in the park.

5   Oak ash beech sycamore and elm are deciduous trees.

6   My favourite football teams are Everton Arsenal Motherwell Newcastle and Linfield.

Adverbs

A Complete each sentence by putting in the right **adverb** from the list below.

1 Snow fell _____heavily_____ on the mountain.

2 The girls ran _____quickly_____ down the hill.

3 Anne slept _____soundly_____ after her long swim.

4 Our team won the swimming gala _____easily_____ this year.

5 The sun shone _____brightly_____ all morning.

6 The old man walked _____slowly_____ up the stairs.

7 Bill bought his bicycle _____cheaply_____ at the sale.

8 The hungry dog ate his food _____greedily_____ .

brightly	**greedily**	**quickly**	**cheaply**
heavily	**easily**	**slowly**	**soundly**

B Add an **adverb** to complete each sentence.

1 Derek tied the rope _____trickily_____ .

2 Ali behaved very _____strangely_____ .

3 Grandma could not cross the road _____easily_____ .

4 The nurse treated her patient _____nicely_____ .

5 When our team scored we all cheered _____happily_____ .

6 I can do those sums _____too joyfully_____ .

7 Tom painted his picture _____beautifully_____ .

8 The crane lifted the steel bars _____gently_____ .

Vocabulary and spelling (1)

A The answers to these clues all end in **ey**.

1 Used to open a lock. _k_ _e_ _y_
2 Bees make this sweet food. _h_ _o_ _n_ _e_ _y_
3 Like a small horse with big ears. _d_ _o_ _n_ _k_ _e_ _y_
4 Bank notes and coins. _m_ _o_ _n_ _e_ _y_
5 Smoke goes up one. _C_ _h_ _i_ _m_ _n_ _e_ _y_
6 A small animal that lives in hot lands. _m_ _o_ _n_ _k_ _e_ _y_

B The answers to these clues all end in **aw**.

1 A metal blade with teeth for cutting. _s_ _a_ _w_
2 An animal's foot with claws. _p_ _a_ _w_
3 Dry stalks of cut corn. __ __ __ __ __
4 Everyone must obey the _l_ _a_ _w_.
5 The lower part of your face. _j_ _a_ _w_
6 To make a picture of something. _d_ _r_ _a_ _w_

C The answers to these clues all end in **le**.

1 A two-wheeled vehicle. _b_ _i_ _c_ _y_ _c_ _l_ _e_
2 A fruit. _a_ _p_ _p_ _l_ _e_
3 A bird of prey. _e_ _a_ _g_ _l_ _e_
4 A gun with a long barrel. _r_ _i_ _f_ _l_ _e_
5 Burned to give light. _c_ _a_ _n_ _d_ _l_ _e_
6 A referee uses one. __ __ __ __ __ __

Adjectives (1)

A   Write out the **adjectives** in these sentences.

1   Jayne wore a pink dress at her party.

2   Our football team wear blue shirts.

3   A big lorry skidded in the snow.

4   Mark played with his new game.

5   The rabbit hid in the long grass.

6   A tall policeman helped the old lady to cross the road.

7   The tall cupboard was full of old books.

8   "Don't walk on the wet floor!" shouted the grumpy caretaker.

9   The long, thin rope was tied round the fat man's legs.

10   The huge tanker was rolling in the rough sea.

B   Match each of the **adjectives** in column A with the **nouns** in column B.

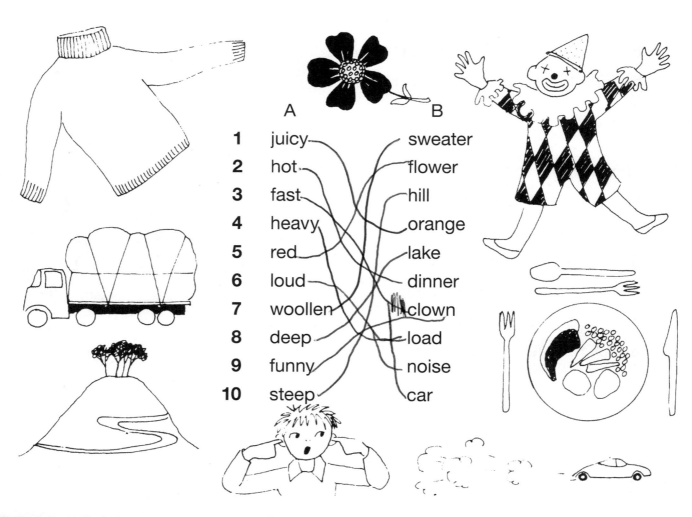

	A		B
1	juicy		sweater
2	hot		flower
3	fast		hill
4	heavy		orange
5	red		lake
6	loud		dinner
7	woollen		clown
8	deep		load
9	funny		noise
10	steep		car

Pictures and sentences

Write a sentence about each picture.

There are some words to help you.

1 dad — spade — garden

2 girl — bicycle — kerb

3 dog — cat — garden

4 farmer — pigs — sty

5 mum — baby — pram — pond

6 boy — fence — trousers — nail

7 lighthouse — rocks — rough — ship

8 boy — bounce — pavement — car

Alphabetical order (1)

a   b   c   d   e   f   g   h   i   j   k   l   m

n   o   p   q   r   s   t   u   v   w   x   y   z

A   Write each list of words in **alphabetical order**.

1	bark	bench	bold	big	bull
2	acorn	air	above	animal	arrow
3	cut	chess	camel	crow	clock
4	place	puzzle	paint	pram	pencil
5	skin	shed	seven	sail	seal
6	duck	door	desk	dart	dig
7	milk	music	meat	money	make
8	tent	thief	talk	tomato	tie
9	wheat	wasp	wrist	week	wife
10	rhyme	rust	real	rain	ribbon

B   Write the word(s) which is **out of order** in each of these lists of words.

1	lamb	leaf	lion	lunch	log
2	nail	nine	netball	note	nurse
3	fall	fell	fill	fox	floor
4	earth	echo	eel	eight	edge
5	germ	ghost	giant	gold	glue
6	help	hymn	hide	hole	hutch
7	jungle	jam	jeans	jigsaw	joke
8	vest	village	valley	volcano	vulture
9	paint	pearl	pillar	present	past
10	dentist	dwarf	diamond	dollar	drill

Joining sentences (1)

A Use **who** or **which** to join these sentences.

Remember: **who** for **persons**

which for **things.**

1 Here is the girl. She is a good swimmer.

2 I caught the dog. It bit the boy.

3 The teacher praised Tom. He had written an exciting story.

4 I thanked the policeman. He found my bike.

5 We travelled on the train. It went to Cardiff.

6 Jim caught a fish. It was swimming in the pond.

7 This is my aunty. She lives in Belfast.

8 Mrs Rigby has two sons. They are very tall.

B Choose **so** or **but** or **because** to join each pair of sentences.

1 Tim slipped and fell. He did not hurt himself.

2 She had measles. She could not go to school.

3 Brenda returned the shoes to the shop. They were too small.

4 The hotel was burned down. No lives were lost.

5 She could not speak. She had a sore throat.

6 The garage was closed. We could not buy any petrol.

7 We went to the forest. We wanted to see a woodpecker.

8 The policewoman chased the dog. She did not catch it.

Gender

A   Write the missing words.

	male	female			male	female
1	prince	....	6	bridegroom	....
2	man	....	7	father	....
3	boy	....	8	wizard	....
4	uncle	....	9	grandfather	....
5	son	....	10	god	....

B   Write the missing words.

	male	female			male	female
1	....	actress	6	....	waitress
2	....	mayoress	7	....	widow
3	....	queen	8	....	she
4	....	niece	9	....	heroine
5	....	sister	10	....	wife

C   Write the missing words.

	male	female			male	female
1	....	lioness	6	....	cow
2	gander	....	7	fox	....
3	....	doe	8	....	ewe
4	stallion	....	9	cock	....
5	....	tigress	10	....	hind

Verbs (2)

A   Find the **verbs** in these sentences.

1   The boy kicked the ball.

2   Sandeep ran down the street.

3   Tim jumped over the fence.

4   The car skidded on the ice.

5   The baby crawled on the rug.

6   Paul ate his tea and then played cricket.

7   The farmer cut the hedges and fed the cows.

8   The queen waved when we cheered her.

9   Sam cut his leg when he fell off the wall.

10   Our cat purrs when I stroke him.

B   Write down **two** actions which each of these persons might do.

1	your teacher	**6**	a farmer
2	a police officer	**7**	a joiner
3	a nurse	**8**	your mum
4	a soldier	**9**	a footballer
5	a cricketer	**10**	your caretaker

Adjectives (2)

A Complete the following sentences by using the most suitable **adjective** from the list.

1 The .... lights of the car dazzled me.

2 The .... girl fell over the stool.

3 It took Jayne a long time to do the .... sums.

4 The .... kitten chased the ball of wool.

5 A .... cloud usually brings rain.

6 The car skidded on an .... patch on the road.

7 Our chimney blew down in the .... weather.

8 Jack was a .... boy and did not do his homework.

~~difficult~~	windy	~~bright~~	lazy
~~dark~~	clumsy	~~icy~~	~~playful~~

B Rewrite the following groups of words, choosing an **opposite** to the **adjective** in each group.

e.g. a **bright** light → a **dull** light

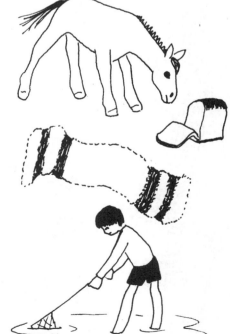

1   a short day   →

2   a sad girl   →

3   a slow train   →

4   a dry towel   →

5   a young horse   →

6   a stale loaf   →

7   a weak lion   →

8   a sour apple   →

9   a shallow pond   →

10 a tame animal   →

11 a wrong answer   →

12 a polite girl   →

Plurals

Write the correct **plurals** of these words.

A
1. dog *dogs*
2. boxe *boxes*
3. brush *brushes*
4. girl *girls*
5. hand *hands*
6. glasse *glasses*
7. match *matches*
8. lake *lakes*
9. fox *Foxes*
10. flower *glowers*

B
1. holiday *holidays*
2. city *city's*
3. army *army's*
4. boy *boys*
5. key *keys*
6. story *stories*
7. monkey *monkeys*
8. pony *ponies*
9. lady *ladies*
10. valley *vallies*

C
1. half *halves*
2. cargo *cargoes*
3. loaf *loaf's*
4. thief *thiefs*
5. potato *potatoes*
6. wolf *wolves*
7. volcano *volcanoes*
8. leaf *leaves*
9. elf *elves*
10. tomato *tomatoes*

D
1. day *days*
2. scarf *scarves*
3. chief *cheives*
4. lily *lilys*
5. child *children*
6. church *churches*
7. piano *pianos*
8. woman *women*
9. foot *feet*
10. paper *papers*

Pronouns

Remember: a **pronoun** is a word used in place of a **noun**.

A   Write out the **pronouns** in these sentences.

1   <u>I</u> am now nine years old.

2   <u>He</u> jumped over the fence.

3   <u>She</u> baked a large cake.

4   Please pass <u>me</u> a ruler.

5   <u>They</u> are going to the cinema.

6   <u>You</u> must eat all your dinner.

7   <u>We</u> enjoyed the party. Did <u>you</u>?

8   There is a dog called Kim. <u>It</u> is an Alsatian.

B   Write out these sentences and put a **pronoun** in place of the **noun** or **nouns** in bold type.

1   **Jasmin** won the first race.

2   **The dog** ran off when I opened the door.

3   **Pat** and **Sue** are busy painting.

4   **The rain** is still pouring down.

5   Peter chose the **flowers** for his mother.

6   **Mr Ahmed** dug his garden.

7   Oliver gave stamps to **Mrs Kay.**

8   Tom asked **Will** for some sweets.

| it | he | they | she | him | her | them |

Adjectives (3)

A Use the vowels **a e i o u** to complete these **adjectives**.

very unkind	c r __ __ l
angry, wild	f __ __ r c __
kind, showing friendship	f r __ __ n d l y
not costing much money	c h __ __ p
not making any sound	s __ l __ n t

B In each line write out the **adjective** which **best** describes the word in heavy type.

1	**elephant**	hungry	huge	tiny	quick
2	**tree**	square	purple	iron	leafy
3	**fire**	blazing	happy	damp	wet
4	**chair**	three-legged	playful	comfortable	sleepy
5	**horse**	smiling	bold	grassy	fast
6	**water**	wet	fresh	loud	woollen
7	**street**	busy	grassy	broken	speedy
8	**gale**	calm	small	howling	warm
9	**orange**	oblong	juicy	green	musical
10	**book**	babbling	lazy	wooden	exciting

C Complete each sentence by choosing a suitable **adjective**.

1 We were very happy when we heard the _____ news.

2 The fireman received a medal for his _____ act.

3 The old lady stumbled along carrying a _____ bag.

4 The boat overturned in the _____ sea.

5 Jess enjoyed eating the _____ pear.

17

Picture comprehension (2)

Look carefully at the four pictures. Write two sentences about each picture so that you tell the story. Give your story a title.

These words will help you.

man	dig	garden	kettle	bird	eggs	
cat	fence	pounce	table	hatched	pleased	

Vocabulary and spelling (2)

A   The answers to these clues all have **tt** in them.

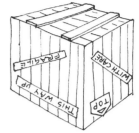

1   Opposite of top.   __ __ t t __ __

2   Bad.   __ __ t t __ __

3   A small room in the roof.   __ t t __ __

4   A food made from milk   __ __ t t __ __

5   A small country house.   __ __ t t __ __ __

6   Nice to look at.   __ __ __ t t __

B   The answers to these clues all have **rr** in them.

1   A looking glass.   __ __ r r __ __

2   Not wide.   __ __ r r __ __

3   The day after today.   __ __ __ __ r r __ __

4   To go quickly.   __ __ r r __

5   A soft, juicy, red fruit.   __ __ __ __ __ __ __ r r __

6   Used with a bow for shooting.   __ r r __ __

C   The answers to these clues all have **ll** in them.

1   Dancing to music on a stage.   __ __ l l __ __

2   A small bird with a forked tail.   __ __ __ l l __ __

3   The colour of buttercup flowers.   __ __ l l __ __

4   High.   __ __ l l

5   A dog wears one round its neck.   __ __ l l __ __

6   A small area where people live.   __ __ l l __ __ __

Contractions

A   Join each pair of words together and write the short form.
Remember: the **apostrophe (')** goes where the missing letter **(i)** was.

1	he is	**5**	that is
2	she is	**6**	where is
3	it is	**7**	what is
4	who is	**8**	there is

B   Join each pair of words together and write the short form.
Remember: the **apostrophe (')** goes where the missing letters **(wi)** were.

1	we will	**4**	she will
2	he will	**5**	I will
3	you will	**6**	they will

C   Join each pair of words together and write the short form.

1	we are	**4**	we have
2	I am	**5**	they have
3	they are	**6**	I have

D   Write these short forms in full.

1	doesn't	**6**	I'm
2	weren't	**7**	that's
3	haven't	**8**	they'll
4	we'll	**9**	when's
5	they're	**10**	can't

Groups

A Choose a group name from the list below to complete each line.

1 bear   kangaroo   tiger   monkey   → Mammals

2 blue   red   green   yellow   → colours

3 spanner   saw   plane   hammer   → tools

4 lemon   peach   strawberry   orange   → fruit

5 van   car   lorry   taxi   → vehicles

6 June   October   May   December   → months

7 sycamore   willow   beech   oak   → trees

8 shark   cod   plaice   sardine   → fish

9 daffodil   pansy   daisy   snowdrop   → flowers

10 robin   sparrow   thrush   duck   → birds

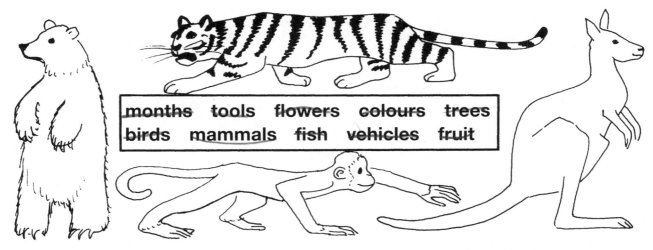

months   tools   flowers   colours   trees
birds   mammals   fish   vehicles   fruit

B In each of the following lines one word **does not** belong to the same groups as the others.
Write the odd word.

1 oak   ash   tulip   beech   sycamore

2 England   Jamaica   Canada   Asia   Egypt

3 peach   strawberry   apple   carrot   lemon

4 tulip   daffodil   buttercup   pansy   grass

5 lorry   ship   car   van   bus

6 carpet   stool   chair   bench   settee

7 horse   hen   donkey   cow   sheep

8 knee   ankle   elbow   wrist   face

Verbs (3)

Write out the following sentences by choosing the most suitable **verb** from the brackets.

1   Tim was (pulled/thrown) off his bike when it hit the kerb.

2   Chantal (walked/limped) off the field after she twisted her ankle.

3   Paul (stepped/leaped) on to the path as the lorry skidded towards him.

4   When the thunderstorm started we (went/dashed) for shelter.

5   The dinghy's sail was (ripped/pulled) to shreds by the raging gale.

6   The express train (travelled/thundered) through the station.

7   The soldiers (walked/marched) smartly to the palace.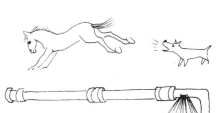

8   The racing cars (drove/roared) along the straight at 260 km/h.

9   The scared pony (lashed/kicked) out at the snapping dog.

10 The water (gushed/dripped) from the burst pipe.

11 The brave man (went/dived) into the sea to rescue the little girl.

12 The thief (snatched/took) the old lady's handbag.

Picture comprehension (3)

Look carefully at the four pictures. Write a few sentences about each picture so that you tell a story. Give your story a title.

These words will help you.

Mark	**Imran**	**zoo**	**entrance**	**price**	**monkey**
grab	**hat**	**swinging**	**bars**	**elephant**	**keeper**
loaves	**trunk**	**sea lion**	**leaping**	**feeding**	**throwing**

Vocabulary (1)

A Which person would you link with each pair of words?

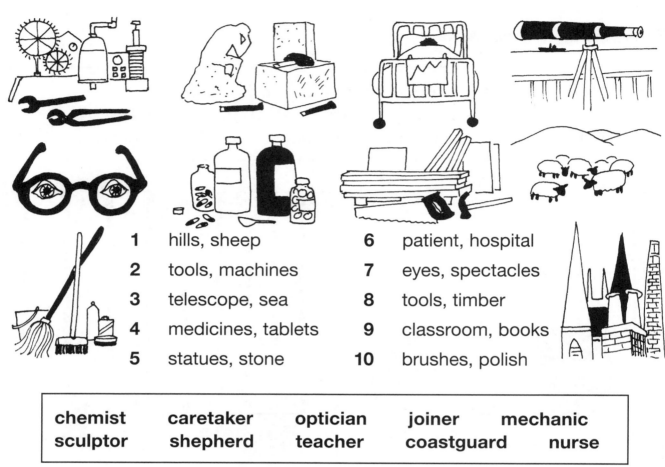

1	hills, sheep	6	patient, hospital
2	tools, machines	7	eyes, spectacles
3	telescope, sea	8	tools, timber
4	medicines, tablets	9	classroom, books
5	statues, stone	10	brushes, polish

chemist	**caretaker**	**optician**	**joiner**	**mechanic**
sculptor	**shepherd**	**teacher**	**coastguard**	**nurse**

B What name do you give to ....?

The first letter of each is given.

1 A person who serves in a restaurant is a w................................. .

2 Someone who draws and paints is an a................................. .

3 The place where bread is made is a b................................. .

4 Someone who looks after your teeth is a d................................. .

5 The place where beer is made is a b................................. .

6 Someone who searches for new lands is an e................................. .

7 A person who repairs leaking water pipes is a p................................. .

8 The place where many apple trees grow is an o................................. .

9 Someone who rides horses in races is a j................................. .

10 A land where very little grows is a d................................. .

Questions

A Use the words from the list to complete the questions.
Don't forget the **question mark (?)** at the end of each question.

1 .... did you put the hamster's food

2 .... is your mother feeling after her operation

3 .... you enjoy your trip to the zoo

4 .... you lend me your bike, please

5 .... of these puppies would you like

6 .... were you not at school this morning

7 .... football boots are these

8 .... would you like to do tomorrow

9 .... you seen the exhibition of models

10 .... said that our team won

Will	**Why**	**Who**	**Have**	**Whose**
Did	**Where**	**Which**	**What**	**How**

B Here are Matthew's answers to some questions.
Write down a question to fit each answer.

1 I live in Sutton, Surrey.

2 My favourite dog is a Dalmatian.

3 No, my sister isn't married.

4 My dad is a joiner.

5 I live on the fifth floor of Tower Flats.

6 Spurs is my favourite football team.

7 Yes, we went to Holland last year.

8 I hope to be an electrician.

9 My mum works in an office.

10 I enjoy football, reading and watching TV.

Similar meanings

A For each word in heavy type write a word which has a **similar** meaning. Choose from the list.

1 Paul found the maths **difficult**.

2 Dad took the **cash** to the bank.

3 Jayne was **weeping** because her dog was lost.

4 The joiner will **repair** the broken fence.

5 The **wealthy** singer drives a Rolls Royce.

6 Do you want me to **assist** you to push your car?

7 Sabrina was glad that her answers were **correct**.

8 Our school concert **commences** at 7.30 p.m.

9 Harvest mice are **small** animals.

10 The plumber is here to **connect** the water pipes.

rich	little	mend	right	hard
join	money	help	starts	crying

B Write out the word in each line which has a **similar** meaning to the word in heavy type.

1	**answer**	shout	reply	whisper	talk
2	**plucky**	strong	shy	brave	lucky
3	**bright**	show	flat	dull	shining
4	**fall**	drop	raise	run	swim
5	**reveal**	have	hide	show	receive
6	**collect**	sweep	gather	clean	jump
7	**short**	dark	tall	brief	long
8	**hide**	seek	ask	show	conceal
9	**sketch**	act	reveal	draw	dance
10	**top**	summit	base	middle	bottom

Adjectives (4)

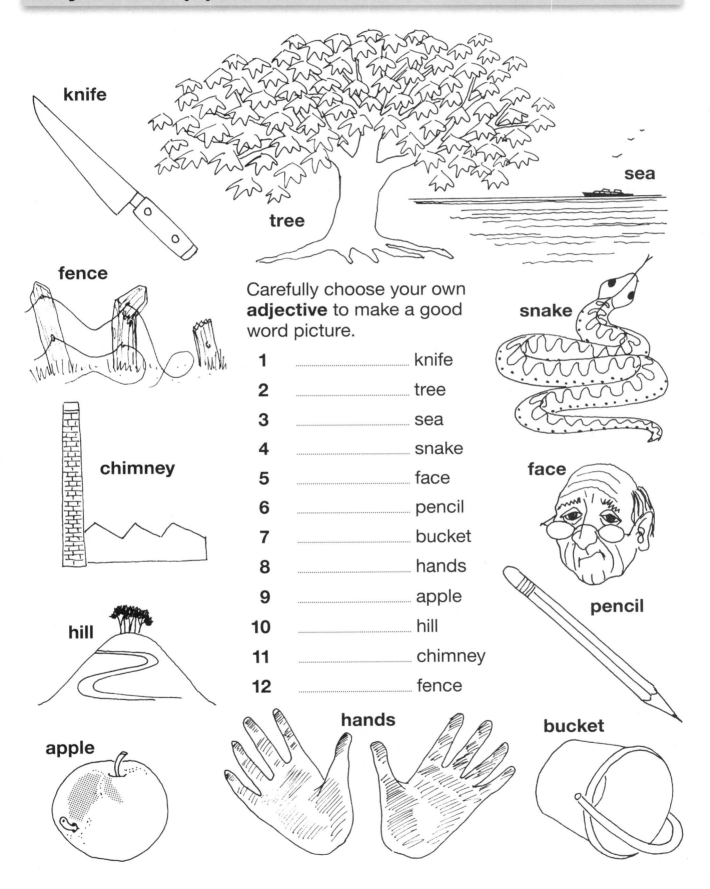

knife

tree

sea

fence

snake

chimney

face

Carefully choose your own **adjective** to make a good word picture.

1 .... knife
2 .... tree
3 .... sea
4 .... snake
5 .... face
6 .... pencil
7 .... bucket
8 .... hands
9 .... apple
10 .... hill
11 .... chimney
12 .... fence

pencil

hill

apple

hands

bucket

Alphabetical order (2)

a   b   c   d   e   f   g   h   i   j   k   l   m

n   o   p   q   r   s   t   u   v   w   x   y   z

A   Write the following words in **alphabetical order**.

1	male	marble	mayor	magic	mast
2	paw	pale	page	parcel	path
3	tap	taxi	tale	table	tadpole
4	walrus	watch	wax	wagon	war
5	bend	berry	bell	beach	bee
6	cage	card	cactus	camel	cabbage
7	date	daffodil	dagger	dawn	dark
8	father	fair	farm	face	fall
9	grab	grow	grease	grunt	grip
10	verb	vehicle	veal	vestry	velvet

B   Write the word(s) which is **out of order** in each of these lines.

1	bible	bicycle	big	bird	bill
2	cigar	cider	cinema	circle	city
3	deaf	deck	dentist	deep	desert
4	weak	web	weed	well	weigh
5	rifle	rice	ring	ripe	river
6	maid	make	mammal	magic	mast
7	hair	hall	hang	hand	hard
8	fear	feet	fed	ferry	fever
9	nail	napkin	naval	nasty	nation
10	shaft	ship	short	shut	shed

Mixed bag (1)

A Choose the correct word from the list to complete each sentence.

1 The football belongs to him. The football is ....

2 The horses belong to them. The horses are ....

3 The book belongs to you. The book is ....

4 The apples belong to us. The apples are ....

5 The bicycle belongs to me. The bicycle is ....

6 The cat belongs to her. The cat is ....

7 I bought a ball. The ball is ....

8 Jade has a new dress. The dress is ....

9 They have some sweets. The sweets are ....

10 You have a dog. The dog is ....

mine	yours	his	ours	hers	theirs

B Complete these sentences by choosing suitable words from the list.

1 His face was as white as ....

2 The miner's hands were as hard as ....

3 Paul's hands were as dirty as ....

4 Helen was as busy as a ....

5 The stray dog was as thin as a ....

6 Joe's hands were as cold as ....

7 The bird's feathers were as green as ....

8 This parcel is as heavy as ....

9 My parcel is as light as a ....

10 Her apple is as sweet as ....

rake	honey	snow	bee	ice
nails	feather	mud	lead	grass

Opposites

A   Write out the word with on **opposite** meaning to the word in capital letters in each line.

1	UNHAPPY	miserable	sad	glad	ill
2	GIVE	present	own	take	have
3	BEGIN	commence	run	end	start
4	GOOD	nice	neat	happy	bad
5	LARGE	small	thin	huge	tall
6	NOISY	shout	row	quiet	scream
7	CLEAN	bathed	dirty	washed	ill
8	HOT	cold	warm	sun	fire
9	DAY	afternoon	dawn	morning	night
10	SHALLOW	small	thin	deep	paddle

B   Write out these pairs of words.
If they are **similar** in meaning write an S after them.
If they are **opposite**, write an O.

1	shout whisper	9	front back
2	stay remain	10	clean pure
3	found lost	11	clean dirty
4	first last	12	rich poor
5	close near	13	fear terror
6	ascend descend	14	bleak dreary
7	separate unite	15	hold release
8	careful cautious	16	colossal gigantic

Comprehension (1)

Eating in the Ice Age

During the Ice Age, people lived very differently to how we do now. They ate some very different foods to what we eat nowadays. They didn't have sugary foods like biscuits, cakes and sweets. Other than fruit, honey was the only sweet thing they ate. They ate lots of honey, which they took from the nests of wild bees. This was risky, as bees can be dangerous in big swarms and can sting.

Some of their diet was the same as ours. They ate lots of fruit and vegetables and they also hunted animals and caught fish so they could eat meat and fish. Ice Age people also ate some things we would never eat today, like caterpillars!

1   Write down four foods that people ate during the Ice Age which we would eat today.

2   What did people during the Ice Age eat which you wouldn't like to eat?

3   Write down three things mentioned in the passage which we eat now but people didn't eat during the Ice Age.

4   What did they eat instead of sugar?

5   Where did they get their honey from?

6   Why was collecting honey risky?

7   How do you think the bees defended their nests?

8   What insects are mentioned in the passage?

Abbreviations

A   Write the **abbreviation** for each of these words.
The list will help you.

1	Avenue		6	August
2	January		7	Terrace
3	Road		8	December
4	September		9	Square
5	Street		10	October

Sept.	Terr.
Ave.	Dec.
Sq.	St.
Aug.	Oct.
Jan.	Rd

B   Write the **abbreviations** for each of the following.

1 Royal Air Force

2 On Her Majesty's Service

3 Doctor

4 Police Constable

5 Post Office

6 Her Majesty's Ship

7 United Kingdom

8 Victoria Cross

9 British Broadcasting Corporation

Verbs (4)

Choose the correct **verb** to complete the sentences.

A **was** or **were**

1 All the boys .... playing football.

2 Not one of the animals .... harmed by the fire.

3 They .... making model planes.

4 Every girl .... in the swimming pool.

B **is** or **are**

1 Anybody .... allowed to borrow a book.

2 Not one of the children .... absent from school.

3 Every one of the bottles .... broken.

4 All the children .... visiting the museum.

C **ate** or **eaten**

1 Sarah had .... all her sweets.

2 The greedy dog .... his food very quickly.

3 Many cabbage leaves had been .... by caterpillars.

4 Jade .... an apple on her way to school.

D **broke** or **broken**

1 A football .... the classroom window.

2 This window has been .... twice before.

3 Beth said that she had .... the vase.

4 The vase .... when Beth bumped into the table.

Vocabulary (2)

A Complete the following. The list of words will help you.

1   a _____ of pups   8   a _____ of fish

2   a _____ of sheep   9   a _____ of books

3   a _____ of bees   10 a _____ of trees

4   a _____ of people   11 a _____ of flowers

5   a _____ of cattle   12 a _____ of wolves

6   a _____ of sailors   13 a _____ of soldiers

7   a _____ of teachers   14 a _____ of ships

---

herd   crew   forest   litter   pack   fleet   swarm
bouquet   flock   regiment   library   crowd   staff   shoal

B Complete these sentences.

1   Bananas, mangoes and plums are all types of _____ .

2   Freesias, lilies and carnations are all types of _____ .

3   Salmon, tuna and herring are all types of _____ .

4   Rubies, emeralds and sapphires are all types of _____ .

5   Beetles, flies and grasshoppers are all types of _____ .

C What would you expect to find:

1   in a kettle?   9   in a safe?

2   in an envelope?   10   in a hutch?

3   in a library?   11   in a garage?

4   in a vase?   12   in a sty?

5   in a gallery?   13   in a wardrobe?

6   in an aviary?   14   in a wallet?

7   in a greenhouse?   15   in a dustbin?

8   in a hangar?   16   in an aquarium?

Joining sentences (2)

Choose the best word from the list to join each of the two short sentences.

A

so	when	where	but	while

1 I went to the shed. I found a frightened puppy.

2 Mary was sleeping. We were playing.

3 It was muddy. We put on our wellingtons.

4 She did her best. She did not win the prize.

5 Jake was climbing a tree. He saw the fire.

B

but	before	so	because	which

1 This is our secret cave. It is full of surprises.

2 David could not drink his tea. It was too hot.

3 Jenny looked for her kitten. She could not find it.

4 Sam began to shiver. He put on his coat.

5 Abdul had a bath. He went to bed.

C

but	though	while	who	yet

1 We saw the policewoman. She saved a lady from drowning.

2 The wind was very cold. It was the month of June.

3 Andrew was very clever. He was lazy.

4 Evie could not climb the rope. She tried her best.

5 Mark made a fire. Andrew put up the tent.

Vocabulary and spelling (3)

A   The answers to these clues all have **ce** in them.

1   He helps to keep law and order.   __ __ __ __ c e __ __ __

2   A teacup stands on one.   __ __ __ c e __

3   A large lump of ice that floats in the sea.   __ c e __ __ __ __

4   Part of something.   __ __ __ c e

5   A house for a king or queen.   __ __ __ __ c e

6   Two times, or double.   __ __ __ c e

7   Doing something many times.   __ __ __ __ __ __ c e

8   A time when there is no war.   __ __ __ c e

B   The answers to these clues all have **tch** in them.

1   A small clock, usually worn on your wrist.   __ __ t c h

2   The room where food is prepared and cooked.   __ __ t c h __ __

3   A home for a pet rabbit.   __ __ t c h

4   A field used for playing football.   __ __ t c h

5   A mark made with something sharp.   __ __ __ __ t c h

6   Looking at.   __ __ t c h __ __ __

7   To sew with thread.   __ __ __ t c h

8   Used by some people to help them walk.   __ __ __ t c h __ __

C   The answers to these clues all have **ck** in them.

1   A machine for telling the time.   __ __ __ c k

2   A covering for the foot and leg.   __ __ c k

3   To hit with the foot.   __ __ c k

4   A summer game.   __ __ __ c k __ __

5   A young farm bird.   __ __ __ c k __ __

6   A short coat.   __ __ c k __ __

7   Cups, saucers and plates.   __ __ __ c k __ __ __

8   Worn on a chain round the neck.   __ __ c k __ __ __ __

Comprehension (2)

One Saturday Afternoon

It was a glorious Saturday afternoon, and the sun was shining from a clear blue sky. Thomas was sprawled out on the bed, his t-shirt damp against his skin. He turned the page of his book and asked his brother Joshua to open the window a bit more.

Joshua was standing at the upstairs window looking into the garden and the fields beyond. He could see mum, tall and elegant, leaning casually on the flimsy fence and sipping a cold glass of lemonade as she chatted enthusiastically to Mrs Henderson next door. Mrs Henderson was small, round and had a big mane of wild frizzy white hair that she had tried to pull back into a ponytail. She was sweating too.

He pushed the window open as far as it would go.

1   Which room was Thomas in and what was he doing?

2   Who was in the room with Thomas?

3   Did the boys live in a house or a bungalow? How do you know?

4   What was the neighbour called?

5   Write two things that describe mum.

6   Write two things that describe the neighbour.

7   Why do you think Thomas asked Joshua to open the window?

8   Do you think mum liked the neighbour?

9   What season of the year do you think it was?

10   Why do you think Thomas's t-shirt was damp?

The apostrophe – ownership (1)

A Write out the following using the **apostrophe (')** to show there is **one owner**.
e.g. David's book

1	the babys toy	**9**	the referees whistle
2	Daniels bike	**10**	the horses tail
3	the firefighters helmet	**11**	Carolyns car
4	the dogs kennel	**12**	the giraffes neck
5	the birds feathers	**13**	the cars tyres
6	the deers antlers	**14**	the lions claws
7	the rabbits ears	**15**	the gorillas cage
8	the teachers table	**16**	the police officers radio

B Write these the short way.
e.g. the spade which belongs to Sam → Sam's spade

1 the pen belonging to Mark →

2 the pram belonging to Jess →

3 the tent which belongs to Adam →

4 the heat of the sun →

5 the garage of the car →

6 the coat belonging to mum →

7 the cage of the parrot →

8 the petals of the flower →

9 the caravan belonging to Mr Brown →

10 the tail of the cat →

Vocabulary (3)

A   In each of the following groups, write out the one word which includes all the others.

1	girls	men	people	boys	women
2	Moscow	Paris	London	Brussels	capitals
3	apple	fruit	date	orange	pear
4	cabbage	lettuce	turnip	vegetables	cauliflower
5	supper	breakfast	dinner	tea	meals
6	football	cricket	tennis	sports	squash
7	table	furniture	chair	cupboard	bookcase
8	drum	recorder	piano	organ	instruments
9	vehicles	van	bus	taxi	lorry
10	Glasgow	Belfast	cities	Swansea	Leeds

B   In each of the following groups, arrange the words in the order of size of the object, beginning with the smallest.

1	rat	sheep	rabbit	horse	elephant
2	minute	week	second	day	hour
3	wren	starling	ostrich	seagull	turkey
4	city	village	house	country	continent
5	puddle	ocean	lake	sea	pond
6	cup	bath	kettle	eggcup	bucket
7	trunk	tree	twig	branch	leaf
8	shark	goldfish	cod	whale	shrimp
9	metre	millimetre	kilometre	centimetre	
10	yacht	liner	dinghy	rowing boat	supertanker

Verbs (5)

A Begin each of these sentences with **Yesterday** and change the verb to the past tense.
e.g. Jamila **wins** the race.
  Yesterday Jamila **won** the race.

1 The dog **plays** in the garden.

2 The baker **bakes** a lot of bread.

3 The trawler **sails** into the open sea.

4 Peter **arrives** at school at nine o'clock.

5 The farmer **chases** the dogs away from the sheep.

6 Paul **takes** a long time to do his maths.

7 Dad **drives** his car to the garage.

8 Tim **flies** his model aeroplane.

9 Charlotte **feels** ill.

10 Our teacher **reads** a story to the class.

B Change the **verb** in bold type to show that something happens or is happening now.

1 The girl **spoke** with an American accent.

2 The boy **rubbed** his sore knee.

3 The thrush **hopped** about looking for worms.

4 Sarah always **found** time for reading.

5 Josh **brought** his young brother to school.

6 The dog **sat** outside the shop door.

7 The cars **stopped** at the traffic lights.

8 The workmen **dug** a deep hole.

9 The dog **begged** for a bone.

10 The bus **skidded** on the ice.

Vocabulary and spelling (4)

A The answers to these clues all have **pp** in them.

1 The last meal of the day.   __ __ p p __ __

2 A fruit.   __ p p __ __

3 Soft, comfortable shoes worn in the house.   __ __ __ p p __ __ __

4 A reddish metal.   __ __ p p __ __

5 A herring dried over smoke.   __ __ p p __ __

6 A hot-tasting powdered spice.   __ __ p p __ __

7 To come into sight.   __ p p __ __ __

8 A small greyhound.   __ __ __ p p __ __

B The answers to these clues all have **gg** in them.

1 Cases and baggage used by a traveller.   __ __ g g __ __ __

2 Turning over the soil.   __ __ g g __ __ __

3 Someone who does throwing and balancing tricks.   __ __ g g __ __ __

4 A short, sharp knife.   __ __ g g __ __

5 The largest.   __ __ g g __ __ __

6 To fight with something or someone.   __ __ __ __ g g __ __

7 To laugh in a silly way.   __ __ g g __ __

8 Rough and sharp at the edge.   __ __ g g __ __

C The answers to these clues all have **dd** in them.

1 To walk in shallow water.   __ __ d d __ __

2 When people get married.   __ __ d d __ __ __

3 The place where someone lives.   __ d d __ __ __ __

4 The centre.   __ __ d d __ __

5 A seat on a horse or a bicycle.   __ __ d d __ __

6 A small, poisonous snake.   __ d d __ __

7 Happening quickly.   __ __ d d __ __ __ __

8 To interfere with something.   __ __ d d __ __

Rhyming words

A Write out the word which **rhymes** with the word in bold type.

1	**pail**	fall	pill	sale	wall	fell
2	**pot**	goat	note	top	lit	knot
3	**die**	bee	high	say	may	lay
4	**done**	fun	sum	phone	wrong	gone
5	**pour**	our	low	for	fur	hour
6	**you**	bough	how	flew	bow	though
7	**frost**	post	lost	most	boast	toast
8	**bone**	none	sun	lone	won	bun
9	**care**	fear	here	fur	purr	hair
10	**knew**	bow	know	few	low	knot

B Write the missing word in each line. It must **rhyme** with the word in bold type.

1 **bawl** A wren is a _____ bird.

2 **floor** Will you please _____ me a cup of tea?

3 **seat** I shall _____ you outside the Post Office.

4 **bean** Have you _____ my cat anywhere?

5 **flour** The rose is my favourite _____ .

6 **white** I went to bed late last _____ .

7 **fair** It is rude to _____ at anyone.

8 **might** I must _____ a letter to my pen friend.

9 **seek** Pam was _____ after her long illness.

10 **date** I had to _____ an hour for the bus.

The apostrophe – ownership (2)

A Write out the following using the **apostrophe (')** to show that there is **more than one owner**.

1 the ladies hats
2 the dogs dinners
3 the police officers boots
4 the soldiers guns
5 the sheeps tails
6 the footballers shirts
7 the childrens books
8 the insects wings

9 the firefighters hoses
10 the foxes cubs
11 the mices tails
12 the sailors ship
13 the womens shoes
14 the boys changing room
15 the cats kittens
16 the teachers books

B Write these the short way.
e.g. the trunks of the elephants
        the elephants' trunks

1 the club for children
2 the cage of the wolves
3 the cloakrooms for pupils
4 the library for children
5 the staffroom for teachers
6 the dressing rooms of the footballers
7 the fangs belonging to the snakes
8 the meeting of the workers
9 the clothes for ladies
10 the babies of the parents

Improving sentences

A   In place of each **adjective** in heavy type choose another from the list which will improve the sentence.

1   The **hungry** dog was trapped for six days in a cave.

2   The Jumbo jet has **big** engines.

3   **Large** waves crashed over the ship caught on the rocks.

4   The pyramids are **old** buildings in Egypt.

5   The climber was trapped on the **dangerous** cliffs.

6   It is very **moist** in the jungle.

7   The fox is said to be a **sly** animal.

8   The man's **odd** behaviour puzzled us.

ancient	**cunning**	**humid**	**powerful**
enormous	**strange**	**starving**	**perilous**

B   'The man dived into the water to rescue the boy.'

By using **adjectives** this sentence can be made more interesting.

'The **brave** man dived into the **deep** water to rescue the **terrified** boy.'

Improve these sentences by adding suitable **adjectives**.

1   Last winter we had _____ snow, _____ frosts and _____ gales.

2   The _____ clowns wore _____ costumes at the circus.

3   Yesterday I saw a _____ man trying to cross a _____ road.

4   I enjoy a _____ apple after my lunch.

5   The _____ motorist drove slowly in the _____ fog.

6   The _____ sheepdog rounded up the _____ sheep.

7   I saw the _____ firefighters rescue two _____ children from the _____ house.

8   The _____ monkey climbed down the _____ tree and grabbed the _____ girl's ice cream.

Compound words

A Write the name of each picture. Show the two words which form the
compound word.
e.g. bull + dog → bulldog

B Now use each word in a sentence.

Mixed bag (2)

A   Complete the following with a suitable **noun**.

1   Uncle is to nephew as aunt is to _____ .

2   Foal is to horse as lamb is to _____ .

3   Hat is to head as shoe is to _____ .

4   Honey is to bee as milk is to _____ .

5   Sound is to ear as taste is to _____ .

6   Ear is to hear as eye is to _____ .

7   Sing is to bird as bark is to _____ .

8   Table is to wood as window is to _____ .

B   Which **verb** in the brackets means the **opposite** of the word in heavy type?

1   **move**   (run   gallop   halt   race   walk)

2   **receive**   (have   buy   give   sell)

3   **arrive**   (come   depart   stay   enter)

4   **conceal**   (hide   reveal   bury   place)

5   **climb**   (ascend   scale   soar   rise   descend)

6   **repair**   (mend   break   make   alter)

7   **shut**   (fasten   lock   close   open)

8   **defend**   (protect   attack   help   support)

C   Complete each sentence with an **adverb** made from the word in brackets.

1   The horse was galloping _____ towards the gate.   (quick)

2   The nurses _____ lifted the injured boy.   (careful)

3   The aeroplane landed _____ with a damaged engine.   (safe)

4   Tommy wrote his story very _____ .   (neat)

5   Grandad nodded his head _____ .   (sleepy)

6   The tortoise moved _____ across the grass   (slow)

7   The boys were working _____ on their canoe.   (busy)

8   The lions roared _____ at their trainer.   (angry)

Similar sounding words

Write out the sentences, completing them by choosing the correct word from the brackets.

1 My football cost £3 in the .... at the sports shop.   (sale, sail)

2 You must .... your brother outside school.   (meet, meat)

3 The bus .... to town is now 50p.   (fair, fare)

4 Sally was in .... when she broke her arm.   (pain, pane)

5 Mark looked .... when he was ill in bed.   (pale, pail)

6 Our house is on a busy .... road.   (mane, main)

7 A .... tree hasn't any leaves.   (bear, bare)

8 The football team lost .... first match today.   (their, there)

9 Please bring your book ....   (hear, here)

10 The car was too .... so dad didn't buy it.   (dear, deer)

11 We went on the dodgems at the ....   (fare, fair)

12 A lion has a long ....   (main, mane)

13 The .... on the yacht was torn by the strong wind.   (sale, sail)

14 The .... is a timid animal.   (dear, deer)

15 A .... is a kind of bucket.   (pale, pail)

16 John kicked the ball which broke a .... of glass.   (pain, pane)

17 I don't think the .... is cooked enough.   (meat, meet)

18 The polar .... eats a lot of fish.   (bare, bear)

19 Put the bicycle ....   (there, their)

20 Don't shout! I can .... you.   (hear, here)

Answers

Page 2 Verbs (1)
A 1 – 10 Check your child's words.
B 1 – 10 Check your child's words.

Page 3 Nouns
A 1 horse **2** chocolate **3** water **4** apple **5** dinner **6** police officer, thief **7** cat, roof **8** boys, girls, cinema **9** Leaves, tree **10** books, library
B 1 – 10 Check your child's answers.
C Check your child's answers.

Page 4 Picture comprehension (1)
Check your child's words are appropriate.

Page 5 Punctuation
A Check your child's use of capital letters and full stops.
B 1 The Jumbo jet landed safely.
2 Have you seen our new caretaker?
3 A tortoise has a hard shell.
4 We enjoyed Tim's party.
5 Will you play football with me?
6 Did you see that unusual bird?
7 Our lawn needs cutting.
8 Why don't you eat your dinner?
C 1 The butcher sells lamb, beef, chicken and sausages.
2 The cricket season is May, June, July, August and September.
3 The sailor had been to China, Japan, India and Australia.
4 I saw snowdrops, crocuses, daffodils and tulips in the park.
5 Oak, ash, beech, sycamore and elm are deciduous trees.
6 My favourite football teams are Everton, Arsenal, Motherwell, Newcastle and Linfield.

Page 6 Adverbs
A 1 Snow fell **heavily** on the mountain.
2 The girls ran **quickly** down the hill.
3 Anne slept **soundly** after her long swim.
4 Our team won the swimming gala **easily** this year.
5 The sun shone **brightly** all morning.
6 The old man walked **slowly** up the stairs.
7 Bill bought his bicycle **cheaply** at the sale.
8 The hungry dog ate his food **greedily**.
B 1 – 8 Check that your child's adverbs are appropriate for the sentences.

Page 7 Vocabulary and spelling (1)
A 1 key **2** honey **3** donkey **4** money **5** chimney **6** monkey
B 1 saw **2** paw **3** straw **4** law **5** jaw **6** draw
C 1 bicycle **2** apple **3** eagle **4** rifle **5** candle **6** whistle

Page 8 Adjectives (1)
A 1 pink **2** blue **3** big **4** new **5** long **6** tall, old **7** tall, old **8** wet, grumpy
9 long, thin, fat **10** huge, rough
B 1 juicy orange **2** hot dinner **3** fast car **4** heavy load **5** red flower **6** loud noise
7 woollen sweater **8** deep lake **9** funny clown **10** steep hill

Page 9 Pictures and sentences
1 – 8 Check that your child's sentences describe the pictures.

Page 10 Alphabetical order (1)
A 1 bark, bench, big, bold, bull
2 above, acorn, air, animal, arrow
3 camel, chess, clock, crow, cut
4 paint, pencil, place, pram, puzzle
5 sail, seal, seven, shed, skin
6 dart, desk, dig, door, duck
7 make, meat, milk, money, music
8 talk, tent, thief, tie, tomato
9 wasp, week, wheat, wife, wrist
10 rain, real, rhyme, ribbon, rust
B 1 lunch, log **2** nine, netball **3** floor, fox **4** eight, edge, ei **5** gold, glue **6** hymn **7** jungle
8 valley **9** past **10** dwarf

Page 11 Joining sentences (1)
A 1 Here is the girl **who** is a good swimmer.
2 I caught the dog **which** bit the boy.
3 The teacher praised Tom **who** had written an exciting story.
4 I thanked the policeman **who** found my bike.
5 We travelled on the train **which** went to Cardiff.
6 Jim caught a fish **which** was swimming in the pond.
7 This is my aunty **who** lives in Belfast.
8 Mrs Rigby has two sons **who** are very tall.
B 1 Tim slipped and fell **but** he did not hurt himself.
2 She had measles **so** she could not go to school.
3 Brenda returned the shoes to the shop **because** they were too small.
4 The hotel was burned down **but** no lives were lost.
5 She could not speak **because** she had a sore throat.
6 The garage was closed **so** we could not buy any petrol.
7 We went to the forest **because** we wanted to see a woodpecker.
8 The policewoman chased the dog **but** she did not catch it.

Page 12 Gender
A 1 princess **2** woman **3** girl **4** aunt **5** daughter **6** bride **7** mother **8** witch
9 grandmother **10** goddess
B 1 actor **2** mayor **3** king **4** nephew **5** brother **6** waiter **7** widower **8** he **9** hero
10 husband
C 1 lion **2** goose **3** buck **4** mare **5** tiger **6** bull **7** vixen **8** ram **9** hen **10** stag

Page 13 Verbs (2)
A 1 kicked **2** ran **3** jumped **4** skidded **5** crawled **6** ate, played **7** cut, fed **8** waved,
cheered **9** cut, fell **10** purrs, stroke
B Check your child's answers.

Page 14 Adjectives (2)
A 1 bright **2** clumsy **3** difficult **4** playful **5** dark **6** icy **7** windy **8** lazy
B 1 a long day **2** a happy girl **3** a fast train **4** a wet towel **5** an old horse
6 a fresh loaf **7** a strong lion **8** a sweet apple **9** a deep pond **10** a wild animal
11 a right/correct answer **12** a rude girl

Page 15 Plurals
A **1** dogs **2** boxes **3** brushes **4** girls **5** hands **6** glasses **7** matches **8** lakes **9** foxes **10** flowers

B **1** holidays **2** cities **3** armies **4** boys **5** keys **6** stories **7** monkeys **8** ponies **9** ladies **10** valleys

C **1** halves **2** cargoes **3** loaves **4** thieves **5** potatoes **6** wolves **7** volcanoes **8** leaves **9** elves **10** tomatoes

D **1** days **2** scarves **3** chiefs **4** lilies **5** children **6** churches **7** pianos **8** women **9** feet **10** papers

Page 16 Pronouns
A **1** I **2** He **3** She **4** me **5** They **6** You **7** We, you **8** It

B **1** She **2** It **3** They **4** It **5** them **6** He **7** her **8** him

Page 17 Adjectives (3)
A cruel, fierce, friendly, cheap, silent

B **1** huge **2** leafy **3** blazing **4** comfortable **5** fast **6** wet **7** busy **8** howling **9** juicy **10** exciting

C **1** Check your child's adjectives.

Page 18 Picture comprehension (2)
Check that your child's sentences explain what is happening in the pictures.

Page 19 Vocabulary and spelling (2)
A **1** bottom **2** rotten **3** attic **4** butter **5** cottage **6** pretty

B **1** mirror **2** narrow **3** tomorrow **4** hurry **5** strawberry **6** arrow

C **1** ballet **2** swallow **3** yellow **4** tall **5** collar **6** village

Page 20 Contractions
A **1** he's **2** she's **3** it's **4** who's **5** that's **6** where's **7** what's **8** there's

B **1** we'll **2** he'll **3** you'll **4** she'll **5** I'll **6** they'll

C **1** we're **2** I'm **3** they're **4** we've **5** they've **6** I've

D **1** does not **2** were not **3** have not **4** we will **5** they are **6** I am **7** that is **8** they will **9** when is **10** cannot

Page 21 Groups
A **1** mammals **2** colours **3** tools **4** fruit **5** vehicles **6** months **7** trees **8** fish **9** flowers **10** birds

B **1** tulip **2** Asia **3** carrot **4** grass **5** ship **6** carpet **7** hen **8** face

Page 22 Verbs (3)
1 thrown **2** limped **3** leaped **4** dashed **5** ripped **6** thundered **7** marched **8** roared **9** kicked **10** gushed **11** dived **12** snatched

Page 23 Picture comprehension (3)
Check that your child's sentences explain what is happening in the pictures.

Page 24 Vocabulary (1)
A **1** shepherd **2** mechanic **3** coastguard **4** chemist **5** sculptor **6** nurse **7** optician **8** joiner **9** teacher **10** caretaker

B **1** waiter/waitress **2** artist **3** bakery **4** dentist **5** brewery **6** explorer **7** plumber **8** orchard **9** jockey **10** desert

Page 25 Questions

A 1 Where did you put the hamster's food?
2 How is your mother feeling after her operation?
3 Did you enjoy your trip to the zoo?
4 Will you lend me your bike, please?
5 Which of these puppies would you like?
6 Why were you not at school this morning?
7 Whose football boots are these?
8 What would you like to do tomorrow?
9 Have you seen the exhibition of models?
10 Who said that our team won?
B 1 – 10 Check that your child's questions are appropriate for the answers given.

Page 26 Similar meanings

A 1 hard **2** money **3** crying **4** mend **5** rich **6** help **7** right **8** starts **9** little **10** join
B 1 reply **2** brave **3** shining **4** drop **5** show **6** gather **7** brief **8** conceal **9** draw **10** summit

Page 27 Adjectives (4)

1 – 12 Check that your child's adjectives are suitable.

Page 28 Alphabetical order (2)

1 magic, male, marble, mast, mayor
2 page, pale, parcel, path, paw
3 table, tadpole, tale, tap, taxi
4 wagon, walrus, war, watch, wax
5 beach, bee, bell, bend, berry
6 cabbage, cactus, cage, camel, card
7 daffodil, dagger, dark, date, dawn
8 face, fair, fall, farm, father
9 grab, grease, grip, grow, grunt
10 veal, vehicle, velvet, verb, vestry
B 1 bill, bird **2** cigar, cider **3** dentist, deep **4** well, weigh **5** rifle, rice **6** magic **7** hang, hand **8** feet, fed **9** naval **10** shed

Page 29 Mixed bag (1)

A 1 his **2** theirs **3** yours **4** ours **5** mine **6** hers **7** mine **8** hers **9** theirs **10** yours
B 1 snow **2** nails **3** mud **4** bee **5** rake **6** ice **7** grass **8** lead **9** feather **10** honey

Page 30 Opposites

A 1 glad **2** take **3** end **4** bad **5** small **6** quiet **7** dirty **8** cold **9** night **10** deep
B 1 O **2** S **3** O **4** O **5** S **6** O **7** O **8** S **9** O **10** S **11** O **12** O **13** S **14** S **15** O **16** S

Page 31 Comprehension (1)

1 Four foods that Ice Age people ate which we eat today are meat, fish, fruit and vegetables.
2 They ate caterpillars, which wouldn't be nice to eat.
3 Three things that Ice Age people didn't eat but which we eat are biscuits, cakes and sweets.
4 Honey was used instead of sugar.
5 They got their honey from the nests of wild bees.
6 Collecting honey was risky because the bees are dangerous in swarms.
7 Bees defend themselves by stinging.
8 Bees and caterpillars.

Page 32 Abbreviations

A 1 Ave. **2** Jan. **3** Rd **4** Sept. **5** St. **6** Aug. **7** Terr. **8** Dec. **9** Sq. **10** Oct.
B 1 RAF **2** OHMS **3** Dr **4** PC **5** PO **6** HMS **7** UK **8** VC **9** BBC

Page 33 Verbs (4)

A 1 were **2** was **3** were **4** was
B 1 is **2** is **3** is **4** are
C 1 eaten **2** ate **3** eaten **4** ate
D 1 broke **2** broken **3** broken **4** broke

Page 34 Vocabulary (2)

1 litter **2** flock **3** swarm **4** crowd **5** herd **6** crew **7** staff **8** shoal **9** library **10** forest
11 bouquet **12** pack **13** regiment **14** fleet
B 1 fruit **2** flowers **3** fish **4** jewels/gems **5** insects
C 1 water **2** a letter **3** books **4** flowers **5** paintings **6** birds **7** plants **8** aeroplanes
9 money **10** a rabbit **11** a car **12** a pig **13** clothes **14** money **15** rubbish **16** fish

Page 35 Joining sentences (2)

A 1 I went to the shed **where** I found a frightened puppy.
2 Mary was sleeping **while** we were playing.
3 It was muddy **so** we put on our wellingtons.
4 She did her best **but** she did not win the prize.
5 Jake was climbing a tree **when** he saw the fire.
B 1 This is our secret cave **which** is full of surprises.
2 David could not drink his tea **because** it was too hot.
3 Jenny looked for her kitten **but** she could not find it.
4 Sam began to shiver **so** he put on his coat.
5 Abdul had a bath **before** he went to bed.
C 1 We saw the policewoman **who** saved a lady from drowning.
2 The wind was very cold **yet** it was the month of June.
3 Andrew was very clever **but** he was lazy.
4 Evie could not climb the rope **though** she tried her best.
5 Mark made a fire **while** Andrew put up the tent.

Page 36 Vocabulary and spelling (3)

A 1 policeman **2** saucer **3** iceberg **4** piece **5** palace **6** twice **7** practice **8** peace
B 1 watch **2** kitchen **3** hutch **4** pitch **5** scratch **6** watching **7** stitch **8** crutches
C 1 clock **2** sock **3** kick **4** cricket **5** chicken **6** jacket **7** crockery **8** necklace

Page 37 Comprehension (2)

1 Thomas was in the bedroom reading a book.
2 Joshua was in the room with Thomas.
3 They lived in a house because they were upstairs.
4 The neighbours' name was Mrs Henderson.
5 Mum was tall and elegant.
6 Mrs Henderson was small and round and had frizzy white hair.
7 Because he was hot.
8 Yes, because she was talking enthusiastically.
9 It was summer.
10 Thomas's t-shirt was damp because he was sweating.

Page 38 The apostrophe – ownership (1)

A 1 the baby's toy **2** Daniel's bike **3** the firefighter's helmet **4** the dog's kennel **5** the bird's feathers **6** the deer's antlers **7** the rabbit's ears **8** the teacher's table **9** the referee's whistle **10** the horse's tail **11** Carolyn's car **12** the giraffe's neck **13** the car's tyres **14** the lion's claws **15** the gorilla's cage **16** the police officer's radio

B 1 Mark's pen **2** Jess's pram **3** Adam's tent **4** the sun's heat **5** the car's garage **6** mum's coat **7** the parrot's cage **8** the flower's petals **9** Mr Brown's caravan **10** the cat's tail

Page 39 Vocabulary (3)

A 1 people **2** capitals **3** fruit **4** vegetables **5** meals **6** sports **7** furniture **8** instruments **9** vehicles **10** cities

B 1 rat, rabbit, sheep, horse, elephant
2 second, minute, hour, day, week
3 wren, starling, seagull, turkey, ostrich
4 house, village, city, country, continent
5 puddle, pond, lake, sea, ocean
6 eggcup, cup, kettle, bucket, bath
7 leaf, twig, branch, trunk, tree
8 shrimp, goldfish, cod, shark, whale
9 millimetre, centimetre, metre, kilometre
10 dinghy, rowing boat, yacht, liner, supertanker

Page 40 Verbs (5)

A 1 Yesterday the dog **played** in the garden.
2 Yesterday the baker **baked** a lot of bread.
3 Yesterday the trawler **sailed** to the White Sea.
4 Yesterday Peter **arrived** at school at nine o'clock.
5 Yesterday the farmer **chased** the dogs away from the sheep.
6 Yesterday Paul **took** a long time to do his maths.
7 Yesterday Dad **drove** his car to the garage.
8 Yesterday Tim **flew** his model aeroplane.
9 Yesterday Charlotte **felt** ill.
10 Yesterday our teacher **read** a story to the class.

B 1 The girl **speaks/is speaking** with an American accent.
2 The boy **rubs/is rubbing** his sore knee.
3 The thrush **hops/is hopping** about looking for worms.
4 Sarah always **finds** time for reading.
5 Josh **brings/is bringing** his young brother to school.
6 The dog **sits/is sitting** outside the shop door.
7 The cars **stop/are stopping** at the traffic lights.
8 The workmen **dig/are digging** a deep hole.
9 The dog **begs/is begging** for a bone.
10 The bus **skids/is skidding** on the ice.

Page 41 Vocabulary and spelling (4)

A **1** supper **2** apple **3** slippers **4** copper **5** kipper **6** pepper **7** appear **8** whippet
B **1** luggage **2** digging **3** juggler **4** dagger **5** biggest **6** struggle **7** giggle **8** jagged
C **1** paddle **2** wedding **3** address **4** middle **5** saddle **6** adder **7** suddenly **8** meddle

Page 42 Rhyming words

A **1** sale **2** knot **3** high **4** fun **5** for **6** flew **7** lost **8** lone **9** hair **10** few
B **1** small **2** pour **3** meet **4** seen **5** flower **6** night **7** stare **8** write **9** weak **10** wait

Page 43 The apostrophe – ownership (2)

A **1** the ladies' hats
2 the dogs' dinners
3 the police officers' boots
4 the soldiers' guns
5 the sheep's tails
6 the footballers' shirts
7 the children's books
8 the insects' wings
9 the firefighters' hoses
10 the foxes' cubs
11 the mice's tails
12 the sailors' ship
13 the women's shoes
14 the boys' changing room
15 the cats' kittens
16 the teachers' books
B **1** the children's club
2 the wolves' cage
3 the pupils' cloakrooms
4 the children's library
5 the teachers' staffroom
6 the footballers' dressing rooms
7 the snakes' fangs
8 the workers' meeting
9 the ladies' clothes
10 the parents' babies

Page 44 Improving sentences

A **1** The **starving** dog was trapped for six days in a cave.
2 The Jumbo jet has **powerful** engines.
3 **Enormous** waves crashed over the ship caught on the rocks.
4 The pyramids are **ancient** buildings in Egypt.
5 The climber was trapped on the **perilous** cliffs.
6 It is very **humid** in the jungle.
7 The fox is said to be a **cunning** animal.
8 The tramp's **strange** behaviour puzzled us.
B Check that your child has used suitable adjectives to complete the sentences.

Page 45 Compound words

A **2** wheel + barrow = wheelbarrow
3 water + fall = waterfall
4 butter + fly = butterfly
5 wind + mill = windmill
6 trap + door = trapdoor
7 port + hole = porthole
8 arm + chair = armchair
9 tooth + brush = toothbrush
10 black + board = blackboard
11 light + house = lighthouse
12 cup + board = cupboard
B Check your child's sentences.

Page 46 Mixed bag (2)

A **1** niece **2** sheep **3** foot **4** cow **5** tongue/mouth **6** see **7** dog **8** glass
B **1** halt **2** give **3** depart **4** reveal **5** descend **6** break **7** open **8** attack
C **1** quickly **2** carefully **3** safely **4** neatly **5** sleepily **6** slowly **7** busily **8** angrily

Page 47 Similar sounding words

1 sale **2** meet **3** fare **4** pain **5** pale **6** main **7** bare **8** their **9** here **10** dear **11** fair
12 mane **13** sail **14** deer **15** pail **16** pane **17** meat **18** bear **19** there **20** hear

Published by Collins
An imprint of HarperCollins*Publishers* Ltd
1 London Bridge Street
London
SE1 9GF

Browse the complete Collins catalogue at
collins.co.uk

First published in 1978
This edition first published in 2012

© Derek Newton and David Smith 2012

10 9 8 7 6

ISBN 978-0-00-750544-9

British Library Cataloguing in Publication Data.
A catalogue record for this publication is available from the British Library.

Project managed by Katie Galloway
Production by Rebecca Evans
Page layout by Exemplarr Worldwide Ltd
Illustrated by A. Rodger
Printed in Great Britain by Martins the Printers

MIX
Paper from
responsible source
FSC C007454

This book is produced from independently certified FSC™ paper to ensure responsible forest management.

For more information visit:
www.harpercollins.co.uk/green